Dancers in Daylight

By Anthony Howell

POETRY

Inside the Castle 1969
Imruil 1970
Oslo: a Tantric Ode 1975
Notions of a Mirror 1983
Why I May Never See the Walls of China 1986
Howell's Law 1990
First Time in Japan 1995
Sonnets 1999
Selected Poems 2000
Spending 2000

FICTION

In the Company of Others 1986

PROSE

The Analysis of Performance Art 1999
Serbian Sturgeon 2000

AS EDITOR

Near Calvary: The Selected Poems of Nicholas Lafitte 1992

Anthony Howell
Dancers in Daylight

POEMS 1995–2002

ANVIL PRESS POETRY

Published in 2003
by Anvil Press Poetry Ltd
Neptune House 70 Royal Hill London SE10 8RF
www.anvilpresspoetry.com

Copyright © Anthony Howell 2003

This book is published with financial assistance
from The Arts Council of England

Designed and set in Monotype Ehrhardt by Anvil
Printed and bound in England
by Cromwell Press, Trowbridge, Wiltshire

ISBN 0 85646 364 7

A catalogue record for this book
is available from the British Library

ACKNOWLEDGEMENTS

'Border Country' was commissioned by the Hay-on-Wye Festival
and appeared in *Border Country: Poems in Process*, Woodwind
Publications; 'Not Getting On' appeared in *Hato-Yo Magazine*,
Japan, and also in *Ambit*; Hermitage was anthologised in *The
Exact Change Yearbook*, Boston; 'Phone' was first published in
Ambit; 'Beautonia' and 'Progress' appeared in *Transcatalog*,
Serbia; 'Aroma of Life' was published in *The Scotsman*; 'Bridge'
appeared in *The Poetry Review*; 'Dancers in Daylight' came out in
The Swansea Review; 'Lost Children' appeared in *The Times
Literary Supplement*; 'Durdle Door' and 'Friesians' both came out
in *Rattapallax*, New York.

CONTENTS

3 *View of a Road*

October

FRIESIANS

Curious cows in modernist hides
Come sinking into the mud to breathe and drink.
They twitch their petal-shaped ears

With clips and tags in them. Tongues flick
Up to bare nostrils. Under long lashes
They roll their oily spheres at us.

When they slurp they start the ball-cock's hiss.
They nudge flies from wrinkles, mount each other's backs,
Squirting jets of grass.

Drooling and blowing in groups,
They approach only to back away from
The offer of a salty hand to lick.

Their patches are like maps of other worlds.
They kick their sides and fret their tails
Beside eight hundred years of brooding church.

DURDLE DOOR

I could have been that spindly boy
In chancery to another there – not strong enough
To break his grip, and yet refusing
To give up. Even then I used to like
The chocolate soil that springs the turf
On the walk down from the camping site,
But estimated the Centurion raised
Upon its plinth above the pebbly beach.
Today I find more violence in the sea
Than in that relic of a war before my time.
These waters cut up rough, except in that small cove
The swimmers use from May until September.
Only there they float in dinted rings
As larger ripples overwhelm the gap
By the white dot of a gull on top of a rock.
The wave's a thing to wrestle on the other side
Where duller patches on the sea's
Expansive skin get swept away by dazzle.
Here the field is sliced in half. Beneath,
Approached by dicey steps, the sea churns
And pulverises chalk. Don't go any closer!
People curl their legs beneath them on the top.
Slabs of grass and cliff slide to the beach's edge
Where weed-entangled wrack slops in the door's armpit.
Lifting ocean surges through its picture frame:
Primary coloured bathers bob against it.
And the wave leaps high in the air, tosses up
Jif bottles and driftwood as if juggling.
Now the sun is reduced to a disk like the moon,

And the flow blackens and races shingle,
Shattering a dog's bark at wings
Which need do nothing to stay up there.
Decked in mermaid garter-belts,
The disciplinarian sea strews whips along the coast,
While two-dimensional men attach themselves to cracks
And lovers climb the skyline for a photo.

QUEENS WEST

Hardly one open shop remains
Inside this draughty vending hall:
It never gets to share the circulation
Of carrier-bagged pedestrians with cash to spare.
Business is so bad that the discount-clothing store
Closes for lunch from eleven till quarter-to-four.
Sometimes its twin flights of escalators function,
Sometimes not, while its mirrors reflect no one,
And most of the shutters are pulled down
In front of premises that went out of fashion
As soon as the new mall opened
On the other side of Queen Street.
That invites immediate penetration
Via portals quite as broad as its facade,
Whereas the merest passageway
Provides the earlier project
With access to its bright and bustling side.
Room, on the lofty levels within,
For forty lavish units, nothing small;
However, a perversion of design
Has caused its enormous plate-glass wall
To advertise their presence on a side-street.
Were it not for some desultory guardianship,
One might ravish an erring secretary
Undisturbed in this vast concrete grot.
It's got more to meditate on actually
Than has your haunt for conventional worship.
Raise your eyes to its uppermost panes:

There a blue vision of happier times
Gets promoted by a wide ribbon of sky
Where buxom clouds go sailing past
Like the bargains that would peel away
From the windows of those rural stores
They've locked and boarded up at last.

BATRACHIANS

A wary nod suffices on the cycle track.
It follows an extensive reach where breezes
Dint the idling river. Clustered round
A sewer's lid, cow-parsley thrives, as muddied
Clouds abet the treacherous stillness of
This prelude to the weir where nothing shows
How such a lazy-seeming stretch accelerates
Before the chute. Slowly the clouds go over
The edge of it onto that wide white slide,
While spinning eddies make a sudden rush
Between protective bars, and concrete ducts
Convey these churning waters into culverts
Open to the gaze below some grills. This
Is where toddlers and teenagers too have been
Seized by the vortex, dragged, as by the hair,
Down to a mesh the surface masks. At trestle
Tables, here, the weir's enthusiasts
May brood, one to a bench, while boys with caps
Turned back glide by, darting glances at
Girls with distant hair, sat on the bank,
Their bikes leant together against a trunk.
But now the loosened water rattles on
Under thickly pelted trees where mallows
With their bloodshot leaves shield the ditch:
In which, stupefaction slows the pace,
But once a fellow seizes on his miss,
He'll stick to his post, in ecstatic state,
Even should his hind legs get cut off.

RIGSBY

For two decades I haven't had the gump
To do more than patch up my butterfly:
Layers of bituminous material remain
Sandwiched between strips of welded metal.
It's one of the Herculean labours of a life
Lived peaceably: stripping a roof to reveal
Very old puddles formed above flashing strips
Pasted over cracks bogged by tile-dust;
Each botched-up job just over-botched again
Like the plaster put on the soiled plaster
Placed on an abscess. Takes a nerve to reveal
My traumatised gutter: rafters dabbed with tar,
Never the right thing done, year after year.
It's hopeless, but there's no stopping him now:
Look at it! He cries, ripping up another sheet
And treading it back on itself. They've overlapped
The lagging incorrectly. It's so bad that
You can't face doing anything about it and it
Gets worse and the wallpaper bellies out beneath.
That's got to go! A hammer claws the battens off.
Gera gets his knees to it. We curse,
And are down to some last shot rags of tarpaulin.
Heave the zinc off the gully for Chrissake
And hear it land in the neighbour's back.
Beneath us I can see the threadbare carpet
Of the lovely room I have never been able
To afford to live in. Looking down on it
Seems theatrical as surgery. As let,
It's up till now been subject to a leak.

BORDER COUNTRY

Whichever route we take, we lose the way:
After the trout-farm, for instance, when the lane
Keeps leading us along the valley floor
Until it hops the stream to climb a while,
Only to descend and re-negotiate
The maze of meadows in the stream's vicinity.
Winding on through alders, then avoiding
Pine and larch plantations, it continues
Dithering until it reaches Llanthony.
Here I doubt the road: it ought to climb,
Since I remember some amazing views;
And so reverse, to turn and then retrace
The single track till Cymyoy reappears,
Its tower askew by landslip or design,
Suggesting how a head should hang aslant
When hands are nailed – and *yoy* is Welsh for yoke.
Above the weathered hamlet which it serves,
The sliding mountain has a yoke-like look:
And where a yoke would dip to fit a neck
Monks on mules brought bitter through the gap
From Longtown which is just across the border.
However, this is not the time to stop:
When I reach the cross-roads, I go left,
Then left again, to crawl behind some ponies
Carrying a trekking party upwards:
Little girls with curls which do not fit
Their velvet-covered riding caps, with glasses
Bouncing on the bridges of their noses.
At the top of this steep stretch of hill
The tarmac peters outs: we're forced to stop,

While the Black Mountains claim the riders.
Now we've got no option but to roll
Down the lane and take the route abandoned.
Right, then right again, and back we go
On tracks we just retraced, and then once more
Along the by-road following the stream,
Slowing at its bends, and backing up
For motorcades descending from the pass
Presumably some distance up ahead of us.
Flitting by a stand of twisted sycamores
We swerve to miss a pheasant, notice bulls
And buzzards, come again to Llanthony,
And pass the point beyond the Half Moon pub
At which I lost my nerve, with Offa's Dyke
Above us on the ridge that marks the border
Separating undulating Hereford
From the bald, escarping hills of Gwent.
Later, though, the blackest hill of all
Bulges at us through a perfect blaze
Of hawthorn blossom slashed at by the wipers.
Rising well above two thousand feet,
This knob is dubbed Lord Hereford's – the Tumpa.
It's a steep, uncompromising bump
Giving the impression of a camel:
Like it, lump it, there's no easy way
To scale the thing, and Dilys says at once,
Derek's mountain! Derek is a painter
Haunted by this gloomy shape: it stumps him
And looms up, an image in his mind
Often seen through such a blaze of hawthorn.
On we go though, since our guiding stream
Winds around it: then we start to climb

On and up and ultimately over
Gospel Pass, to meet the panorama
Taking in both Hereford and Powis
Laid out like one's crumpled bed at breakfast.
Ploughed fields, whale-backed hills, dingles
Moving into ever more be-misted
Visionary vales beyond the Wye
Looping round the bookshop town of Hay.
High above the larches, we are partly
Made of sky, we feel, as we look down:
As if we'd left the ground and joined the blue,
Or balanced on some line between the two.
And later, coming back from Hay, with loot
Sufficient for a bookstall in the boot,
We thunder briefly, as we cross the grid,
Ascending steeply, and encounter mist
Before we reach the ridge: its sluggish density
Has left a chilling trail, a slime of frost
On every mound of turf along its path.
Flakes of snow drift singly to the screen
And disappear. The whiteness keeps us mute.
Rushes mark where moisture leaves the slope,
Otherwise there's nothing to remark
Until the mist gets thinner, which it does
As we come down, to catch the lovely sight
Of many coloured hillsides brushed with snow
Which deepens as each brow begins to curve
Towards the cloud. Across the border now,
I can't believe how aimlessly we drive,
Having eaten well at Ross-on-Wye.
We don't know where we're going, do we though?
My mother can't remember which hotel

My uncle mentioned: something court or grange
Or manor even, in a place called Pen
Or Pen-something, somewhere close to Ross.
Bear in mind my uncle's name is Ross:
I get pretty vexed by our predicament.
When we draw our blank at somewhere grange
One very kind hotelier intervenes
By phoning round and checking out all manner of
Manors, courts, and granges in the area.
Contact made, we sally forth again;
Speeding rather, plummeting down sleigh-runs
Shaped by veering hedges, missing trucks
Lurching at us by so many inches,
Turning minutes later, up a drive.
It leads us to a well-appointed, white
Facade above a golf-course on a slope
Which gradually declines towards a lake.
I'm vague about this, though, because it's raining
Hard when we arrive, and so we scurry
Up the steps and through the double doors
To come across my uncle in the lounge.
We press hands, brush each other's cheeks.
It's true that people shrink at getting old.
My uncle seemed an overbearing tree
When he stooped to let me know the intimate
Facts of life which I already knew
From witnessing how spotted dogs were mated.
He seems darker, shrivelled like a prune,
Or is it just the darkness of the rain?
We sit, though, and manage quite a chat.
He suffers from a squamous type of cancer
Which, he says, sounds to him like squeamish.

This affects the surface of his kidneys.
That's the way it crumbles, I am told.
My cousins now appear with many children:
Chocolate-fingered here, amid the sumptuous
Upholstery, they ruin conversation,
Hide behind the drapes or wander off:
And, simultaneously, my famous cousin,
Who's a tv star and runs a phone-in,
Seems to have mislaid the rubber eye-piece
Off his in-laws' 'steady-cam'. Disaster!
Helpfully I search beneath the skirted
Sofas for a while but can't retrieve it.
Gosh, the gardens here are simply lovely:
Roses climbing over bits of buttress.
How the children would have loved to play here,
Had it not been pouring, as is typical.
My uncle hankers after people though.
He has driven all the way from Crawley
To be here. And yet the children seem
Merely to provide my gilded cousin
With an interference which protects him
From the risk of deeper intimations.
My other cousin snaps when tea is served
And he's supposed to mind a pressing child.
I'm sure I like him all the more for that.
I want to go on chatting with my uncle:
It may be the last chance I get.
His wife says it's practically a miracle
That here he is recovered, almost well.
I don't know – he looks ill to me.
He's advised me many times – on property,
On girlfriends and divorces, and most recently

On my mad mother's passion for her builder.
Now he seems to occupy the border
Between life and death, or so I feel.
Cream tea is a bit much with six
Children in a rather grand hotel.

OCTOBER

The morning after they drive out of Oundle,
Progress to the motorway, then travel
Back to London, past the place across
The barrier where a tail-back several junctions
Long inexorably suspended them
In the biggest row they've had in years:
Tears from her, the ugly, choking sort,
And rage from him, because he *never* cries.
All weekend he's been a prey to wind.
His Datsun moves their silence nearer London,
Both afraid of broaching any subject
Whatsoever; windows tightly shut
To enhance the *Pioneer*'s acoustics
As it blares out jazz against the speed-
Created draught. He presses her to choose
The next cassette. She opts for Bach's *toccata*.
He inserts it into the machine
As they leave the A1 (M) at Harlow,
Picking up the outer ring, and after
Having left that at the second exit
Passes wind without it being heard.
It leaks out underneath his seat. The grand
Themes the master touches on vibrate
The Datsun's chassis, but beneath the sound
The air is fetid and the situation
Hard to take, so ordinary it seems
And stale too, especially while waiting
For the lights to change on reaching Hackney,
And made the more unbearable by music
Structured like the vaulting of a nave.

NOT GETTING ON

Again and again
To discover we do not love each other.

Nothing makes sense so why
Try to make nothing?

Knowing this
You think we deserve a cup of tea?

NOWHERE

Poppies built like vultures
Grip the clay where
There may have been a floor.
Having got this far
By some arbitrary turns,
Persevering in the unspectacular

Hinterland of a small town,
I alarm my new car near
A narrow wartime bridge,
Then hurry to catch up
As you step across a wire
And slip down the crumbling

Side of an old cutting
Onto a disused line.
This bisects a vista,
Leading between hedges
Across a rusted barrier
We negotiate, to go on

Past a fishpond where a man
Whips his rod behind him,
Nearly catching one of us,
Before he casts his line
Onto an inert stretch.
He doesn't care to speak.

We go where once
The rails went though
Their ridge has gone to seed;
Soldier through the tall
Grasses and the heat,
Penetrate a gloomed copse,

To step out into light:
The blackberries practically
Overwhelm our route.
Still we tread gingerly on,
Getting even deeper
Into a shut-down territory:

Pastures truly overgrown;
Marshland where a buzzard wheels
Above the skeleton of an elm.
Now we keep going since it's to be done,
Walking further into a world
In which we're alone,

Where no one seems to have been
For so long we feel alien.
It is the epitome of nowhere
And we have got there.
It could be the very last time
We walk together, anywhere.

RAG OF MANY COLOURS

Possession went both ways with such a charm–invested shawl:
One could lie beneath it like a meadow–covered hill.
Jealousy was prompted, since I needed to cling onto it
Vehemently if someone had the nerve to tug it gently.
Then I woke one morning to discover that my shawl
Had disappeared. Never was awakening more empty.
The object of my love had been transmogrified by conjuring
Into the bland, pink and completely unsuckable rabbit
That stood looking uncomfortable on the back seat of the Anglia.
Later I resisted entering the dark room where a conjurer
Was about to start his tricks, and sabotaged a party.
As for the rabbit, I loathed it, and while distrusting sorcery,
I doubted what my mother said and guessed instead my shawl
Had been abducted. So I tossed the rabbit to the dogs,
And still remain convinced that my mother was the culprit,
Feeling no compunction when I burglarise her hand-bag.
Am I getting my own back, or do I do it largely because
Of a compulsion to spend cash? Not properly considering
What it is I miss the most, I'll hunt for what to buy,
More or less for the rest of my life, graduating from Colts
In holsters to records, tapes and CDs, magazines,
More food than I eat, accessories for the Escort,
More cutlery than I shall ever lay, petite, intriguing
Antiques, innumerable shirts, underpants and socks,
And impulse wear from hospice rails, markets, car-boots,
Vintage stalls, and, on occasion, off-the-peg from Debenhams.

MEN

They set off down the grassy track with the dachshund
At their heels. The viaduct makes a lovely start,
Stretching between parapets. It's a dizzy view they get
When glancing over one of these, for the arches
Shadow a gorge where threads negotiate pebbles.
Now his son runs on and up through woods,
Following a path of roots and quite unstable shale.
He follows far more gravely, the dachshund gamely
Scrabbling behind him. Finally they reach the level
Floor of an abandoned quarry which the boy has
Very nearly scaled. His father and their challenged friend
Go carefully round its drastic edge, only to come upon
Another sheer amphitheatre hollowed out on top of the
        other.
After this it's a short but steep last effort
Up to the brow where an unexpected cavern can be
Got at through a lancet doorway. Yes, inside the hill,
There's a sort of crypt – its vaulted ceiling fluted –
Though it stinks a bit. They both peer apprehensively
Into the dripping gloom of it; hesitate to investigate
The weird orifice, prefer to stand silhouetted,
Very tall and manly, on the mound above this
In a sunlit wind, together with their panting hound,
Commanding all that once industrious valley with its
        viaduct.

LATER

It was only later
That she didn't want to be anywhere,
When, wherever she was,
She wanted to be driven somewhere else.
If she stayed with them
She wanted so to be with him.
But if she left and went to stay with him
Then she longed to be with them.

Helpless, yet intolerant
Of help at either end,
She had already ceased
To admit that she would cease.
Her best friend
Had just been to visit her.
She sighed for him and said
That she wished that he would visit her.

And later, later she sat,
Half in, half out of the seat,
Either getting into the car
Or getting out of it.

FEEBLE FABLE

A lady once secure
Against the sands of time
And the sea beyond,
With half a score
Of labourers retained,
Grew old and then instructed them
To hack down those defences
That stopped the creeping sands
And onslaughts of the sea;
And thus the very hill
Her house was built on
Caved in completely,
Pitching house and lady
Into the sea that sweeps away all time.

TWO PORTRAITS

I   MOTHER

Both retinas malfunction and recalling
Hardly happens, mostly you vent hate
And loathing since it has to be appalling
To have lost the thread of what you state
Before you've got it out, while where you sit
Proves nowhere, which is why you like being driven
Anywhere – and if this seems a bit
Erratic, when few bearings can be given,
That is why you say you hate the side
You're sitting on, but though you may forget
Why, what and where, you're still out for the ride,
And that feels better than being in a fret
About being merely sat, and better yet,
Your dachshund's here for you to pet and chide.

2   SON

Consuming luscious books, éclairs, Bebop's
Immortal tracks – Red Rodney, Johnny Griffin,
Paul Gonsalves – here idles 'Man who shops':
Alone in town, exhausted, having striven
To ensure his fest had fewer flops
Than some which have been celebrated with an
Ever so much larger budget – drops
Asleep inside his car now, having driven
Someone to an airport. Should who pops
Pills and slops his coffee be forgiven
His extravagance this once, who crops
His thinning hair too seldom, all unriven
By a comb, who sits in bars and props
Himself awake, considering full stops?

GRUMUS MERDAE

Yesterday they chose her curtain rail.
He was allowed to bear it out of Homebase.
Isn't he her knight in shining armour?

Finding it too short, he took it back,
Exchanged it for a longer lance, or rather
Two in one more pricey plastic pack.

These will need a double screw between them.
She isn't screwing him. This afternoon,
Having secured a surreptitious key,

He sneaks inside her new house with his builder.
There, upstairs, they assemble and affix
His trophy, which he paid the extra length of.

This ends up cut short and far too high.
Still, they screw the bookcase in her bedroom
To the wall just where she wants it – maybe.

Later, when his madness is brought home to him,
He gets drunk on the cognac meant for her,
Makes horrible apologies, then snaps

Everything, undoing all their screwing.
Lies on the sofa dully after that,
Pierced by the lance of guilt.

FROM A WILDERNESS

Her voice has made love to my ear.
The nightingales heard and fell silent.
I wanted to nourish that voice.
Now I've a thirst for her breath.

Giving her up would be death.
Her voice has made love to my ear.
This is the air of my choice.
The nightingales heard and fell silent.

THE HAPPY MICE

How convenient it must be
To get on so well with the lodger
In her cute white house.
She works on her screen
And he works on his.
Easy going, it's no chore to him
To share her meat-free diet
Or to lend her socks.

When she was ill he
Behaved with such chivalry,
So he deserves what he gets
These cold winter nights.
How nice it must be to be him.
Perhaps she senses that she lives
Under some lucky star.
After all, he can even play the guitar!

Just count up the pips
On their answer-machine.
So many calls! Where
Can they have gone?
Bet they listen to us all
Before deciding who to reply to.
I'll be darned if I find one on mine.
But that's fine. That's fine.

OLIVE'S OIL

Spinach being what it is,
Popeye makes mincemeat of Bluto.
Everything goes smoothly with Olive too.
There was little he had to do
Since she prodded with that elongated toe.
Olive keeps things oiled
With a little help from Wimpy
On Friday nights,
For even if his underwear is soiled,
She has simply to turn off the lights
And fit his only rubber
Which she washes in the sink.
Now she's turning Popeye
Into a proper lubber.
His boat is full of sand
And his eyeball has begun to shrink,
Although he still looks quaint
Rolling on dry land.
Meanwhile what of Bluto? Heck,
He ought to wind Olive
Around Popeye's neck;
Refuse to be well-bred,
Eat a few sharks
And stop sitting on the sea's bed
With his head in his hands,
Marvelling at Popeye's glands,
And how the spinach turns his biceps
Into those extraordinary mounds.

THE PLEASURE OF YOUR COMPANY

Why do we hurt each other so?
My longing to converse with you
Interferes with everything I do.
Now you refuse me any attention:
I could get to the stars with you,
But must accept I merit this oblivion.

Still being steeped in you, I sit
Alone now in my attic, close to tears,
Dwelling on the faces you might pull.
You look so lovely talking, haven't we
Talked on into the wee small hours?
I think of a twisted thread of hairs,

And of your insouciant airs.
When you move your mouth in that
Lopsided way I could die for you,
And though I broke the pact we made
Only to talk, I can't regret
My carrying you upstairs to bed.

What am I to do without the
Pleasure of your company – it being
A pleasure simply to watch you
Talk from the opposite end of a table?
Best to hope my talk may bring you
Pleasure too, and never brood again.

FROM A FATHER

When you have done with being a girl
Please come to me, and if you are ever
Ample and womanly, let me be tender.
Though you are just a landscape to me,
Loved, but far away, thinking of you
Fills me still with so much warmth
And friendliness. I need to feel
The rasp again of your sardonic self.
My craving for reunion matches
Your desire to keep us well apart.
How horrid I have been to you,
Though I was only desperate
To find some way of enchanting you.
Once you seemed quite fond of me,
And now perhaps you feel that I'm
Some nasty sort of glue. But that's untrue.
I shan't conjecture anything of you.

WAITING FOR RESCUE

As tail-winds vibrate my reflective triangle,
I sit here, in a fix, halfway round a corner
On a wet ascent from an underpass
At rush hour. My Escort gets the shakes
With each passing batch of traffic.
Unable to maintain my anticipation of the AA,
I sit with trousers damp, in soaked anorak,
Misted in, behind my inactive wheel.
Breath blurs still further a terminally dull vista,
And there's been no letter, therefore
No missing me, no tail-wind to the memory.

DUE DATE

What a cheat it is:
We allow others
To remind us of ourselves,
Only to lose them
And so lose entire limbs.

NIL BY MOUTH

'My mouth never tries.'
An indomitable friend
Tells me why she cannot be
My naked love again.

Pulse oximeters network
Through connectors
To my mother's mask
Below this frigging sign.

The Garden of Eden

HERMITAGE

A whiff of chestnut squanders afternoon
As laughter overflows the eiderdown.
We are out of step with society,
Making love in a house which resembles a shell
At times when others work. The air is still.
Peonies burst their globes in the little plot
At the back of the house. The windows have no sight.
Above the roof, a tall aerial
Serves as horn and periscope.
Our studies provide us with vessels
For containing our madness: stitches,
Games with beads and the lamination of rubrics
Between coffee and coitus. Then we sleep,
Wasting irrelevant daylight, working through the dark
To the sound of the mile-away train
Heading for its black sun.
Later bed may claim us yet again,
But then I find I scratch inside my head
Among the pit-props, for I lie awake
Flat on my back, still hacking away
At the ghostly bedroom ceiling,
Forever pulling poetry apart
Till trucks below the curtains start.

PLENTY

At long last I pass through the check-out
Into that Golden Age
Where sunlight chafes the foliage
To touch on breasts and flanks,
And following Dionysus
With his timbrels and his pipes,
I ambulate my trolley amid maenads
Moving in the van of plump Silenus
As he lurches on his ass
Between double rows of chariots.

We're heading for places viewed from afar:
Those distant clumps I've longed to explore,
And where the mill-races pour
Into the immensity of lakes as large as skies.
Mown by clean sheep there, a glade
Invites a picnic pillaged from a bagged-up cornucopia
Spilt from the hatch-back parked in Arcadia.

MACALPINE

A giant crane extends its arm
Over this tall block's roofless top.
Down in the street, helmeted builders gaze upwards
As forty-eight sizable timbers
Get lifted off a truck.
A heart-shaped pulley hoists them up
While the walkie-talkied foreman speaks
To an operator winching in its hook.
Next a strap is tested on a stack
Floated off and missing vans,
Then lifted as instructed,
To land without alignment,
Pushing a man off-base, lift again
And lower by fractions of inches.

Away the iron heart swings on its sky-strings
As she unzips and grips her dress
With arms crossed, elbows raised,
Revealing first her tights
And then her stomach as she tugs
And lifts it over her head.

MOONLIGHT SEMESTER

Only the moon is permitted to shine
On this metaphysical campus where retired
Thespians play the roles of intellectuals.
A few hideously deformed geniuses
Go wheeling by, carrying the universe
Inside heads as shapeless as the moon tonight,
While lonely academics moult,
Nesting in the corners of their common-rooms.
Togas are preferred to gowns,
Though jogging shorts are more often worn.
Sentinel litter-bins punctuate
The concrete colonnades, and drinks dispensers
Full of Cokes and Lucozades
Stand at the feet of flights of steps
Currently undergoing alterations
As the campus ramps rumpus gathers speed.
Joggers thread the cloisters where their peers
Are being taught to walk so slowly
No one can see them moving. Only
The moon's misshapen silhouette
Is allowed to fall on the bare white pavers
Outside Graduate College, while the dried
Wings of a sycamore litter the moss
In a nearby precinct where a magpie prates
Before flying off at the approach
Of a sad policeman carrying an easel.
Studious windows reflect nothing but moonlight,
And despite the predominance of animal rights in philosophy,
One alarm is answered by another,
Sulphur wafts from the wing of chemistry,

And willows weep in front of halls of residence.
Dead years dance in a ring around
The sandals of brown sociologists as they
Flap across these squares trailed by wives.
Like some enormous crucible, a skip
Has been dropped in front of the mossy grove
Where students imitate statues.

LOST CHILDREN

A thousand and a thousand more again,
These little waves roll in along the shore,
And constantly appear and disappear
While mothers tear their useless hair.
Calling, calling one more time:
Each vanishment abruptly noticed
With a sick chill, either when
A *paterfamilias* heads for a car-park too soon
Or when Akela stoops to examine
A traction belt too long at the steam fair.
Awful to end up so far ahead of the others
At the Pitch 'n' Putt, only to discover
Your chums have already abandoned the game;
Worse to be left behind at the toboggan run.
And so one calls and calls in vain
Where knee-high marram hides a kink in a track
Up through the dunes where the wartime
Pill-box daubed with obscene requests
Pronounces them bludgeoned or,
No, not yet, they *must* turn up,
Blistered merely by the Wild Parsnip,
At the Lifeguard Service Point, not under sand –
And then the odd one, the simply forgotten,
Missing, but not missed, ekes out an existence
Trawling for bottles on deserted beaches.

MEMORIES OF THE OLD DAYS
IN ADAMSDOWN

The old block has been boarded up
While underneath a tent of plastic sheeting
The newest block is under construction.
Residents of the old block have at last been relocated
To one with superior facilities
Completed late last year. But still
Some of its exes have fondish memories
Of their former quarters. From these
They could peep out over the wall, catching the corner
Of Rumpoles; a tavern flanked by the fire-station forecourt
And by the back of the law-court where
A colossal mosaic of Justice
Glances blindly over her shoulder.
She rides on a band of vigilant eyes,
A blatant, rather vulgar symbol, hidden actually
From the row of small windows
Where they used to poke their feet through the bars
To tan their shins in summer. These
Were always amenable lags, self-motivated
In a way, and even today there's no call for the hangman.
Modernisation brings better plumbing but less
Communication with the world. For there was a time
When any Moll could impose on the forecourt,
Shout up her old man, and parade
Her burgled belly and a fresh young fellow:
''Ere, I'm five months gone – it's 'is!'

THE COOL SISTERS

Their mirrors flood the meadows
As we travel through their shadows
Remarking on the symmetry
Of massive thighs a lash away.

They slide slowly past
Trailing vapours – vast
Vases you can pour
The entire sky into and more.

BATTERSEA

A mauve cloud of impressionism
Drifts across an ice-blue sky.
Cold dark flows beneath the cars.
That mere paring hauls the tide up.

Tall stacks, and no sign of the stars.
A burgeoning smudge of vapour;
One distant pristine pendant;
This river at its zenith.

MOBILITY

Unable to decide quite where to be,
I'm based in the car this Christmas,
Travelling from relation to relation. Think of me
As an eighty horse-power snail
Whose shell goes wherever it's expected.
In between, I make my lar
From fuel bills and burger tissues,
Take the air by breathing through the heater.
Fingers dark with oil, tagged by Rollo foil,
Snug in my own condensation and ensconced
In the bygone odour of myself, I guess I'm well supplied,
What with the jump–leads, the damp–start
And the anti-freeze behind my back,
A trove of coins beneath each rubber mat.
If I require sustenance there's melted peppermint
Pooled in the key tray, crumbs
Of chocolate smeared into the stubble.
These corroded tapes keep me company:
They squeak along to what they play.
Memory's stirred by mud from walks, pebbles
From the shore, emptied nylon packets,
Ticket stubs and someone's glove.
After each lunch, I roll off for the next supper,
Only to drift down some slip-road, screw back the back
Of the seat and cancel out all consciousness
Of getting there, of which route to take, of where I am,
Of where to exit, when to make my entrance . . .

WETNESS

Certain misty places could prove an inspiration.
The thirty foot tassel of ivy dangling from the rock face lip,
Encouragement to look and look again, to choose
A single dank locale, a scene that intensifies one's interest
In what nature, say, may offer up: the cavern with
The low ceiling where the spate slides under the car-park;
A torrent which talks at fissures when intermittently
It becomes visible, babbling over the darker hiss of its skelter
From cave into cave; its utterance quite feasibly
Oracular in a country hidden at the back of reality. Children
Are brought here by the Pied Piper. Red Kites ride over it.
Its waters sluice through splits in the rock
Which madmen, to my mind, explore, worming
Their way down the dragon-holes, learning to employ
The shallowest techniques to squeeze through some obdurate
Sphincter. Not for me, though I may be prepared
To drive through considerable floods for a fun-pool dip;
The rain quite unromantic, anxiously watched by policemen
Under the bridge where it sluices down while the car
Surges slowly ahead. Will I ever get through this
To the sodden chips of the poolside café?
Well, by the time I do I've missed the last waves
Of the day because they've switched off the machine.
Still, the grimness of it all means there's no queue on the spiral
Up to the slide where chill drops drip, when there is,
Unpleasantly from tiny feet onto my balding scalp. But now,
Without pause for thought, I head on down the tube:
Exhilarating at first but then the slide goes black on a curve
And my weight lends me far more momentum
Than is appropriate for loops which seem intent on looping me
Into some truly impossible knot – my god, this is worse than
    a pothole!

THE GARDEN OF EDEN

I never got to the Garden of Eden, where, at the right time of year,
You might pluck fresh grapes from the vine, pick strawberries
Straight off the ground, or gather peaches, plums and nectarines
From its ubiquitous branches. Figs, there were, and fig-leaves,
Not that you needed these in the small plunge-pool with its
    swim-jet
And Jacuzzi. The club itself was started by Roger and Audrey
In the grounds of an established nursery – it remained a garden
    centre
Even in its hedonistic heyday. Before that, the place was originally
Just a field where nudists could relax; its turf surrounded by trees
And hedgerows abounding in sloes and blackberries. Facilities
    were basic,
But the site good for tents, caravans; the trees acting as a natural
    windbreak,
Making the whole area a huge suntrap. By the late nineties, a barn
Had been converted to form a clubhouse. This was equipped with
    a bar,
Though visitors were permitted to bring their own. Roger and
    Audrey
Presided over this last bastion of permissiveness – with satellite tv,
Videos and a music centre. Passing through the clubhouse with its
    log-fire,
You would enter a 3000 square foot converted greenhouse – inside it,
A ten-seater sauna and fruitful produce everywhere. Impromptu
    parties
Took place there, mini-discs provided the catalyst for dancing.
    Dress
Was always optional. Children banned from this indoor garden
    after 8 p.m.
By this time cross-dressing was the thing, even among nudists!
This is why Roger and Audrey started their cross-dressing service.
They kept a selection of lingerie together with wigs, shoes and
    makeup,

Especially for those who occasionally wished to try the get-up
Of the opposite sex, and, if one hankered to serve as their
    maid for the day,
Or for longer, this could be arranged, they said. Later, again
    unclothed,
You might just lie down on some purpose-built table and float
    away
On the current generated by aroma-therapy into some other
    world
– As if the bliss you were in weren't already enough. I never got
To that garden, paradise of Ubaidians, Sumarians and naturists;
Lush and lovely spot where there was bdellium and the onyx
    stone,
And where they grilled spare ribs with only aprons on. I never
    got there,
No, I left it too late. Terry and Jay though were driven there
    in desperation,
Due to some appalling storms in 1998. Terry felt the indoor
    facilities
Were a good idea but spoiled by a lack of maintenance. The
    camping field
Had not had its grass cut in months. By then it was no secret
    that
The Garden of Eden was adult orientated. Even so, reported
    Terry,
They'd had a fairly pleasant time. The regulars were friendly
And there was no pressure at all to join in. Expulsion came
    from exposure
(The News of the World) – exposure led to conviction. Since
    when
Roger and Audrey have gone, to run a hotel in Margate – east
    of Eden indeed.

BIN

I'd say it's only too seldom
One comes across anything
So affirmative as this
Uplifting celebration
Which unfolds so cannily,
That's if you take me
To Groucho's, wine me,
Dine me and improve
My edge, and tell that shit
To get lost while I
Close the deal with Jarvis.

SNOOKERED

Further advice concerning unauthorised borrowing
Is accompanied by a fax demanding
Value of shares in FTSE 100 companies,
In other companies and managed investments,
Plus details of existing borrowing
And regular monthly expenditure: mortgage,
Pension, life assurance, hobbies, interests, fetishes.
The bank shows too much interest while
I seem to have just spent a house. Either ends
Meet but one disappears from sight,
Or one is much in evidence but the ends:
They wave goodbye at the speed of passing trains.

ROSSIANA

They live in the sky. They dance everyday:
Their reason for seeking the ground
The sound of an accordion, their feet which touch
And touch again as the toes release
Their talcum powder spore. Suavely the tango
Changes pace while they remain in place
And cling and waver in the embrace
Before mellifluous Tino Rossi
Wafts them through the bedroom door,
For *a day with you away is not a sunny day;*
The most blue sky sans you
Seems cloud-filled rather than blue,
And all the words get rearranged like steps
They practice between the lifts
Up on the twentieth floor.

ANDANTE MODERATO

The *milonga* and the night are full of complications
Such as the steel ring piercing your navel,
Your longer than average movements and your exceptional
Slimness; such as your fox of hair, your freckled arms
– And other sigh-provoking charms, hidden ones,
But these will do for now, until my girl returns
From the Midlands. She likes you too, you know,
And she doesn't mind me dancing with you,
So let's go *andante moderato*, even though
Our hearts are making love when we step together so.

SIGMUNDA

She was trying to cut off a duck's leg,
But it was really her husband's head
She was hacking at.
Now she lifts her own leg
High in the air on their bed.

TEASE

Her skirt falls backwards, as it were,
When she does a handstand there:
Petite witch with exposed panties,
Knowing precisely what she's up to
And the effect she's having on
One close enough to view the dappling
On each inner thigh, unlike the pair
In the woodcut, walking upside down
Along the highway. Here the skirt stays
Upright, just as each trouser-leg
Says, I will not cooperate with gravity.
Meanwhile the gaze from below
Penetrates cavernous nostrils
And appraises offshoots from the vertical
Foreshortening assumed by uncles
Fairly regaled by their favourite undies.

VENUSBERG

Common to reach out and up, but surprise in a minor key
Is the gift of these weeping trees. Tumbling from the sky,
The maverick beech or the willow displays a peculiar
Tendency downwards, pitches its tent or settles its voluminous
Crinoline below it. Such enclosures provide
Antidotes to open space; creating ideal places
At the fringes of a lawn: trees which have learnt to sigh;
Saturnine exponents of a gloom to be desired,
For those with actual lives share at least the thrill
Of hiding in their richly sheltered recesses:
Memories of musk within some ponderous bell.
Several must recall their compliant debut
Within the intimate heart of a rhododendron thicket.
You should have been fielding but somehow
Got in too deep with your friend to remain
Part of the match at all. Lost in an amorous mountain;
The beech cascading over the bush; the bush containing you
And I guess egging you on with its external trumpery
Inviting a private earthiness. Oh there was sadness of course
At it's being done, but Paradise partakes of a similar melancholy;
So much sweeter, surely, than a merely upright joy.

AT ANCHOR

They make treacherous place-mats,
These double-agents; acting for darkness
As much as for light, using depth
To serve the sky. Their compact buds
Come snaking up from below,
Eventually to open star-bright kernels
To the gaze of day. Their realm
Is the thinnest of skins, their upper
Surfaces dry – an archipelago of plates
Hopped on and off by a fly,
Except where the surface tension
Has given way maybe; smooth,
Flexible tubes going down and down,
As if providing the life-support
System for some doomed freshwater
Kraken stuck in the sludge at the bottom.
Floating trays with nothing on them
But the imagination's tea-cakes;
In-betweens who hide their workings,
Reaching beyond their element:
Votaries to the antithesis of their pond.

KNICKERS

Of saying nothing but the same thing
Again and again and again,
Ask the one who only paints women
In knickers; more specifically
Only paints that part described
By the knickers and a bit above
As well as a bit below them;
Scrupulously depicts the navel,
The folded-over elastic and material
Lovely as the loveliness it hides;
Portrays the rucked-up chemise
Or fluted hem or froth of lace.
He contemplates the veiling of each delta,
The confluence of thighs at that
Immortal niche hidden perhaps by
Lycra or satin or cotton or silk or
Some other exotic flimsy stuff.
Of knickers he can never get enough.
And he is exact about that
And the absence of everything else.
His work examines knickers from
The back and from the front
And has really very little to do
With either the anus or the cunt.

View of a Road

TWO POLAROIDS

1   SATELLITE SHUTTLE

Step lively please, and watch your step
From airport transport-cartons to the lounge.
Flights are served with charts and teats
For bald papooses fixed to fronts;
Their cropped mums and the rest of us
Roped between movable trees in the queue for seats.

2   TWO-WAY FLOW

Bee-like, we accumulate, surge,
Disperse as others amass,
Waiting for the lights to change
To green before they cross.
Cabs bounce over mends.

Dust accumulates. The sea surges
And disperses. We amass wealth
Or wait for a lucky number
To change our star-crossed lives.
Ink flows onto cheques.

THE OBSERVANT SKYSCRAPER

Say they dispense with the blinds.
These windows are put here
To look at them through
As they embrace and make love.

Say they look out, they might witness
Another hot couple embracing,
Or an isolated person
Peeling off a garment.

Pretty intriguing to watchers
About whom the subject remains unaware,
Given those watching
Can choose the right window.

Now the sheer number of windows
Produces the coolest indifference
As to the stare. Their doings
As unlikely to be observed by others

As they have found it difficult
To observe them. Indeed,
Beyond indifference,
The quantity of these gazes

And their anonymity
Renders them abstract,
And, as abstractions,
Intriguing.

These hypothetical peekers
Contribute to their pleasure,
Now performed while
Pressed against the glass.

APRIL ON LONG ISLAND

Like flowers which look good even when
Crushed by storms, what survives is
The wreckage of our thoughts in a land
Of stunning birds and rarified people.
The sleek, well-fed birds, are they really
So bright, or have they simply been painted?
Is that a sculpture or a farm-implement
In the ploughed field? Orange dogs
Bear aloft their bouffant plumes
To jog along the road's raddled edges.
Tread-marks on the long beach, dog-shit
At the sea's edge. The Atlantic
Flat as an airfield – except where it rolls.
Huts rise from hackled brows hiding cold lagoons.
A lone heron lopes across overcast sky,
While small sawn-off Christmas trees
Vibrate against anti-drift fences on the dunes,
And the bleached carapace of a crab
Lies half-submerged beside an isolated pebble.
Somewhere off to the left, a siren moans
For here be gulls the size of pterodactyls,
And paddling deeper into unreachable
Fringes of the lagoon, swans the size of
Cadillacs – reflected in the wet below the rushes.
Inland, that muscular girl who drives
A rusted Plymouth weeds out the beds
Without bending her knees. Yang flames
Of crocuses appear beneath her hands
Though fog may still make ghosts of trees
Or close in on the day. Branches, wires

And weather-vanes get lost in this:
Basket-rings draw zeros on the grey,
While gulls a little denser than the air
Elevate from hedges where the roar
Could be the waves or just some passing car.
The arrows point in two directions at once.

ANATOMY OF LIBERTY

Liberty stands perched upon a star
Which lies grounded on a small island
Close to Wall Street. Her cornerstone was
Laid by the Grand Master of Masons.

Her pedestal doubles her height and
Though her feet are enormous they are
Difficult to see. Visitors go
Up inside her skirt, experience

Her inversion and cannot tell which
Way she faces. Often as busy
As an anthill, she appears serene
From any distance. Her armature

Is anchored deep in her pedestal.
This is a pylon from which hangs the
Internal steel harness which supports
Her molded copper shell. Some water

Leaking through her seams affected her
Uplifted arm, so no one's allowed
Up to her torch now. You can look out
Through the glass in the gaps of her crown,

And from there you can look up or down,
But a Burle surveillance camera
Has been installed in the back of her
Skull in case you do anything wrong.

THE WORLD OUTSIDE

His mufflers are clipped to his helmet,
And his elbows shake as he rides the buck
Of a drill attached by a tube to the
Compressor in his van. A man striped
Red and white, making a hole in the road
Behind striped boards on trestles.
Red flags flap. Across the hooded cars,
People make encapsulated phone-calls.

Everyone is enclosed, but the man at
Work, does the silence of his job
Get at him as it gets at us, eating
In a glass corner and looking out?
People lost in coats wait for coaches.
Leather gloves and stripes vibrate
As the drill chews up the street.

VENETIANS

Facing their pale sheet of parallels,
Think of that letter you couldn't get off:
Feel cut off from the world.

PHONE

People chat, crack
Jokes, put you down,
Want to eat.

GROUND CREW

With tags attached, men stand to drink.
In overalls, ear-caps at the throat,
Each has hung his tea-bag
Over the rim of his plastic cup.
Their skin merges with beards,
With dark glasses, the terminal's
Dome of maroon. Gloves stuffed
Into hip-pockets, resting off a foot,
They grin slowly, stir their cups and smoke,
Or gesture with the hand
Which holds the cup in quiet talk.

BEAUTONIA

The spell was like that bomb
Which deals with humans.
Deep within each wood,
The doves still croon their rumours;
Roses prosper, magically;
Sunflowers soak up heat.
But long ago the water drained
Out of the old stone swimming-pool.
Beauty lies in state.
Nobody sits contemplating
Chess below her castle.
Coffee is prohibited, and visitors
Might comment on the stillness of the boughs,
Were there any visitors.
In these days of national retreat,
There's no escape from endless peace,
Interminable quiet.

AROMA OF LIFE

The sight of old women near death is beginning to prey on my
   mind.
Each of us must die alone, abandoned, no one can come with us,
Even if someone is holding onto a hand, life ebbs from it, and
A person always goes from life alone. But what of the old woman
Clothed in her peasant's black, hunched over herself by the
Pleskevica stall? As you get more feeble, fainter,
You hunch over more and more, bent around your knees like that,
And in the end only your back can be seen, your forehead
Somewhere beneath it, pressed against the pavement, with a
Cardboard box in front of it, as people queue for their meaty
   burgers,
Hot off the grill, wrapped in delicious tortilla-style bread;
And you can add anything you like from the little boxes there:
Crushed paprika, onions, chives, chopped cabbage, chopped
   carrot,
Chopped beetroot, mustard, ketchup, and a simply delicious
Mixture of sour cheese and paprika, which oozes out all over the
Place as you bite into your well-stuffed tortilla and *pleskevica*.

PROGRESS

Opposite the statue of a patriot,
The cracked, curved facade of *Progress*
Bakes in the heat. When not screened
By sun-blinds, its modestly dressed
Displays might be mistaken for exhibits:
Four cuts of suit, three sizes of iron pan,
One sort of plastic-bordered looking-glass
In two familiar geometric shapes;
The 'Star' hand-mixer, the paint-roller,
The only slightly rusted barbecue grill
Holding up one imported mountain bike.
Then there are boxes filled with those
Innovative cubes of sugar which were there
Before the war – a good while before.

Progress really fills one with nostalgia:
Ancient herbal teas, packaged raisins
And Neapolitan wafers adjacent to the window
Which is home to teddy bears from everywhere.
Inside, it's the emporium of the comatose
Where sales-staff outnumber the consumers.
What may be encountered there, causing one to pause?
Three brooms with choice of coloured bristle?
Identical enamel cans and practical
Plastic nappy-liners pale before the
Housecoat in the ladies' fashions section
Where, since the war is only just concluded,
Most of the manikins remain amputated:
You can't mend their sad stumps with sellotape.

1944

The war was over,
But they stayed on at the camp.
Mattresses were provided
And their soup had a hunk of bread.
Sometimes they worked on the stones,
But when the sun came out
They would put down what they were carrying,
Sit beneath a flowering plum
And roll a cigarette.
The blossom wreathed your smoke,
And it was usual to scratch
The last of your lice
And rock on your haunches,
Calmly watching the bulldozers
Push matchsticks into a trench.

RUNNING FOR TITO

And now she is running for Tito,
Sporting a bright red bandana.
He was their beacon – off she goes!

But the flame swept back beside her
Died last year. She is running away
From his day – and the gap gets wider.

DANCERS IN DAYLIGHT

Paris, who the gods love, who desire slays;
Palaces on crater lips, ivy-covered trees.
Paris, and a cave with broken statuary.
Domitia hears how Dom gouged his head out.
Twisted gates, the mouth blocked by stone fall.
Here's the staved-in scallop of a swimming-pool:
A ripe place for chucking out your mattresses.
Paris, and an olive struck; well it might have been
Him in that track-suit, yearning for the West
Near those famous gardens uplifted over Rome.
I had been mooning on the Palatine since 10 a.m.;
Sat at a sunlit banquet in the Flavian House,
Being Statius, looking up in awe
At rafters there no longer. I had traced
Domitian's maze. Could Q. Sulpicius Max
Have mastered its octagonal, commended at eleven
In the games for poets held in AD 94?

Gentle, perpetual anxiety of minor waves
Around the lake: it's only calm offshore.
Statius is looking for sleep, and the Lord
God is towed beyond this margin's rustlings.
When I was the empress I would canter here,
Slip off my Arab, climb to our tryst,
Happy to play Paris-melted Helen till
The daggers bladed downwards, in between
Collarbone and spine. When the corpse was gone,
His fans unstopped the scents which were his signature
To mark his fall against the steps – this ritual
Led to massacre. Kingcups, marigolds,

Ivy over everything, where Paris strolled
When he was all the rage. Which column
Was it which assigned him to his empress
Who desire slays? – having tasted his desire
During days of arbitrary divorce,
While Uncle Dom went ga–ga over Julia.

I overhear the Britons as they're shown into
Her ruined cave: nymphaeum by the shore
Designed for her by architect Rabirius.
Homage here to Homer as a Paris-trove:
Paris now as Paris, now as Priam old;
As Odysseus, then as Circe, wheedling;
Then a swine, and last Domitian's nothing:
Just a torso tumbled by the water's edge;
No head at all, no neck: an ugly, charred
Crater crudely gouged between the shoulders though.
Yes, Dom did that – and, on a later day,
I squarely sat upon this Lord God's rostrum:
Squares and circles of imperial hue enclosed
In circles, then in lozenges of rosy stone
Bordered by some bilious marble foliage.
The emperor had wanted his divorcee back
After he had forced a death by accident.

A boy is trying on a wig too large for him
As dawn reveals a throne against a crater lip:
Sails of light careen across the bowl below
While the reek of game pervades its wooded slope.
Agonothetes in training jog the lacustrine
Circumference of Diana's glass; a lap or so,
And sweat threads designer stubble as they pass

A poet with his tragedy stitched into him.
Blue is the oval of crater-deep water,
Violets and forget-me-nots. Forget me not.
But Julia, just how was that? A stickler,
Dom was appalled he'd got her up the spout:
Supposed her moral guardian, he ordered her
To down a brew designed to put things right.

Out of all fishermen's hearing, further back
Above the shore, up the overgrown sides of the steep
Enchanted crater rife with beasts below a live
Divinity's retreat – his elevated country seat –
The Lord God's safari park, with ingles there
To clamber up to, laughingly lie down in,
Lovingly to kiss the living, candid skin
Of some delicious shoulder. Ledges a hundred
Feet from where the boys have hung a rope
To swing out from an ilex over water in
The afternoon. Just as I decided to lie down
In the Farnese: jacket spread on small
Square of garden closed by privet hedges:
Prone to sleep while breathing aromatic
Breezes from the oranges; girls abask nearby,
And kids at play, or lost in privet mazes.

Paris, who the gods love, as those about to die:
For there were sea-fights on the lake at times;
Times he crushed me back among bee orchids,
Where he slid inside me, hidden softly then
In fissures which we made our own as spectators lined
A flaming lake – some elephantine ship
Applauded roundly while he soundly rammed me.

Thus the crater rang with clash of arms
As I lay in his arms among the orchids there
Enamoured of my dancer, my divinity.
And then I walked again among the Flavians,
Among their sparse foundations, where an emperor
Transformed into a beetle tried to steer
A passage through a magnitude of ruins
In some humble after, who had hopes perhaps
To be that bumbling hornet next, and irritate
The stroller on his desecrated Palatine
Where Cybele's temple sprouts an ilex patch.

Towed by his slaves beyond sight in the mist,
This is the Lord God seeking the solace of
Utter silence. Julia is dead. Turquoise
In the shallows, as it always was, the lake
Is of the tint her eyes were. Ilexes incline
To dip their leaves, to trail these in the water.
Very dark, they make the turquoise brighter.
Wild barley triumphs over column drums:
Only a toe is left of the emperor's effigy.
Death's angel is God's agent who perniciously
Slew Paris on the steps below the gardens here
As heavy, Hellenistic clouds were gathering.
His terror is the terror of our deviance,
And semen mixed with blood will do it perfectly
.

This grubby stone gets booted by the soldiery:
This booted stone was once the head of Paris.
Purple orchids, reddened berries, violets;
Acanthus, ferns and chestnuts, and he came on me,
And then the scent of chestnut blossom smothered us.

And I would twine my snake around a bendy branch
And tell her not to glide into the undergrowth
In case a hawk should stoop – and then I leant
Out and over Rome, against the balustrade
And gazed into the sun as it began to sink
Beyond the Colosseum and the forae there,
Where the balustrade is like an ornate L
Above the Via Sacra and its monuments.

Those daggers bladed downwards as no olive branch
Deflected them: a lovely chestnut struck
By thunderbolt almightiness. The trees
Are full of creepers. In the breeze they trail
Branches to veil the lake's agitation.
Holm oak, and white, white wisteria.
Swans, mallards – most of her nymphaeum
Stopped by stone fall, manna ash and mattresses.
Then I saw *my* dancer on the terrace here,
On the short arm of that L above the Via Sacra.
Sure it was him, well, practically certain:
After all, we'd met before by accident,
Once, outside the Scala, by a traffic-light.

One of my gods for life, but not on high
Except he leapt, this Paris, that Nureyev;
Blossom and the dancer blossom mingled with;
Paris, marble music, perfect star
Shot upwards, elevation as suspense:
My utterly seducer God – my living one
Who never was the Lord God after all;
That Goddish Lord, well, he was merely Dom.
And Rudolf on the terrace, was he worshipping

The Colosseum or the sun? His hands against the stone
Stuck out from a olive track-suit; terrible
How thin he looked. It *couldn't* have been him,
This apparition, knuckles down, palms up:
They were white – as if made of plaster –
Ghosting a dance; the arms not a dancer's.

NOTE   *I was near Rome in April 1991, prospecting in the
Alban Hills for a novel about the life and times of Statius. I vis-
ited the amphitheatre on the crater which holds Lake Albano (the
Mirror of Diana). This amphitheatre is in the grounds of the
Villa Barberini – once Domitian's palace, now the Pope's med-
itative garden. Below it, by the side of the lake, little remains of
the nympheum where Domitia conducted her affair with Paris,
the greatest mime of his age, later assassinated on the steps lead-
ing down from the Farnese Gardens by her imperial husband.
Above these steps, a few months before he died, I had, or imag-
ined that I had, my last encounter with Rudolf Nureyev.*

  *The ancients regarded midday as 'hot and holy', the hour of
ghosts. Looking back now at the incident on the balustrade above
the gardens, I cannot be sure whether I saw my 'apparition'
before or after I went for my siesta among the orange trees. In
any case, how could I have been haunted by the ghost of a person
who was, at the time, still alive?*

89

VIEW OF A ROAD

They seem to be approaching
But in fact they are going away,
And the herd goes ahead of them over the rise
And between the trees at the end of day.
The herdsman turns to watch them,
Letting his beasts amble on as they please,
While she hitches up her skirt
To wade the ford now, with her friend
Lending her a steadying hand.
The cattle are sure of their road
Which winds around the copse
And over an old bridge below,
Then on perhaps, accompanying the swing
Of wooded slopes towards the place
They came from some eternity ago;
But never again will the herdsman catch
Another glimpse so worth his gaze,
For though the herd may head for home
Each evening, nothing stays the same.
The pair will prove as much a dream
As water that has flowed downstream.

CANCELLED FLIGHTS

Eagles used to wheel above this chasm
Not so long ago – unaltered still,
The precipitous face of its stone
Flares in response to the sunset;
Sunset that was Heaven to the anchorite
Protected by the Templars and their citadel;
And long after the intense cavalcade
Of kayaks has passed into shadow
We will be wandering here on our own
'Naked as nature intended'
Under pinnacles of limestone and
Below the thunderbolt eyes of the eagles
In our dreams, but only in our dreams.

BRIDGE

I think I see what you see in the rock:
A rabbit's leaping shadow, then an ox.
They thought they saw what we see in the cleft
Above the gap a stream shares with a draught:
The dewlap, then the muzzle to the left,
The jawbone touched by light above that plant.
We think we see what they saw
– Or what they thought they saw –
The nostrils of a horse, lionesses' eyes, lionesses
Everywhere around their cavern and the bears'
Eyes in each dent; the flanks of a bison
In this fold, that crack. Nothing
Magic about it, apart from what
They saw or thought they saw above an arch
Hewn in the rock by an ox-bow stream;
Lying here all wet, like us perhaps,
But looking out for lionesses, lionesses.

PLAINT

'He sings of a lady whose spore
Has more aroma than sprigs
Of the garrigue, and your
Best gown is covered in twigs!'

FROM QUERIBUS

Ranged below us are the nearest valleys
Threaded by the road which takes us on:
Their dense combes of hardy Southern bushes
Form a bristling fleece that fills all crevices.

Challenging these, the first significant outcrop
Is most definitely a formidable crag:
Arid conduits on it gouge out furrows
Down unwelcoming features into forests.

Beyond this bald, grey fastness there are several
Blue black ridges pushing back
What lies beyond them. Thus they lend depth
To what would already be distance –

Were it not for some further mountains which
Seem the taller summits and the first
To lose their outline then regain it only
To be wreathed in transient formations

Touched by some surviving rills of brightness;
While beyond these overweening heights,
Peaks which are furthest of all and perhaps the grandest
Merge with the mist that blurs another time.

CATHAR COUNTRY

They are here like us at Queribus
And at Peyrepertuse, fiddling with their
Camera batteries, dragging their red setters
Up congested spirals onto views.
When they meet each other unexpectedly
Hyperbolic protests of astonishment
Lose their fizz in about five seconds flat.
And we are here like them, in fact
We are them; indicating unworriedly near
The lightning conductor above some absolute
Drop. And so we gaze down on ourselves
Moving as remorselessly as ants on some gateau
Across the esplanade of a donjon
Belted by curtains of stone. But as we go down,
We fade also from our own recollection,
Even our images leaving these high places
In the grip of those wizened bushes
With the odours we half-recognised.
No transmigration helps nor any afterlife.
It is not for tomorrow's wraiths to haunt antiquities
Since the ticket-office is closed to their memories
And the cornices frequented only by the birds
Whose names they were never too sure of.

THE HOLIDAY

There's camping by a ladder to a roof-rack in the stars
On pine-scented avenues beside the heavy breather.
But everywhere we stop is a hazard for the radio,
So please shove it past your sword and underneath the seat.
The journey takes its toll in back-aches you can get
Massage-bead seat-covers for, in missed exits or
Slip-roads taken when we should have passed them.
Do we want all directions or simply some other direction?
Even one would do. I bought him the sword in a walled town.
Now he tries to riposte with it when technically
He ought to cut and thrust. He can use it on the thistles
Which infest the farm; but now it's to be put away
Since there are chores to be done: the rubbish hefted.
Evening brings a transient glow lit by canvas anterooms,
And crickets chirp to the fugitive hiss of camping-gas.
Then, as dew condenses on outer shell transparencies,
I spread my mat and wish the human motor had a choke.
Converted to my reconditioning mainly by the missionary
Position of my press-ups, I intend to overwhelm beholders:
Never were such flexed locations come across on me.
Dilys whips through her routine as I chivvy George
Zipped within his combat tent, asleep beside his sword.
Now the pinelight scumbles humble circumflexes
Back with their baguettes extruding from their bicycles.
Dilys sharpens her tools, but there isn't time to execute
Such quaintnesses. A fast crawl to the pool bar with
The underwater stools, and we must deconstruct ourselves.
Later, in a crowded cove, we get a shadeless pitch
Where the feeble pegs provided by our fabrications
Buckle when we try to make them penetrate the ground.

Here are tribal caravans with lobbies for their stoves,
And anti-insect neon casting flares of lumination
Over sisters, cousins, aunts and floors of pseudo-parquet.
We get away at dawn, exhausting this infringed-on coast
So fierce about its horns – so burdened by its *bulevars* of
    concrete:
Shorelines everywhere sacrificed to time-share;
Umbrella pines o'er svelte resorts irradiant from roundabouts.
Gentle dunes are overcome more easily by speculation
Than the perches crags provide for hermit millionaires.
On the flat-lands flats amass and floods of souvenirs!
Confining plants to *jardins* here eases plots for parlours
Manicuring smorgasbords; boutiques turned fish-and-chip
    shops.
Where can we erect our poles without a medical service?
Must we end on the nudist rocks frequented, says the guide,
By savage campers? Toilet bunting breezy on all ledges –
In the teeth of placards, posted by a conscientious few,
Beseeching stripped arrivistes to transport their ordures
Up to where binoculars ensure they get collected.
Best to drive bitterly on, towards remote advertisements,
Verandahs falling back as we ascend abruptly now,
Though every corkscrew turn on this opportune promontory
May reveal another infestation of our kind.
In the last possible cove we find a site, and naturally
Morning finds me cranking up my corporeal engine:
Numberless dynamics keep me busy pumping things,
Then I jog with caution to the gym-club on the hill.
For sportive types they're softish, given a funicular
Elevates them to the showers after they have scuba'd.
See-thru flippers undulate a wasp swimsuit down below,
And signify the species with the triggerish harpoon.
Sub-aqua, we've evolved these webbed extensions to the toes,
But flapping on the rugged rocks who'd want to be a duck?

Underwater weeds wave like Disney at the shoals,
And you can reach among these eager minnows in a mask,
Scattering formations in an instant made of darts.
Beached ahead, the blissful Med just nibbles at the citadel
Praised by someone bare below the hammocks of her brassiere.
Cooler now, the post-siesta strand begins to thin,
With love's adherents clinging on as others start to fold:
They roll up and collapse, and, even as the dinghy teeters,
Cash and keys go jingling as flip-flops head for home.
Someone spanks a lilo as the lessening beach expands,
And Dilys stabs at lovely subjects resting napes in smalls
Of backs, and shaking when supports command departure.
People troop to the car-park carrying babes and baby-gear
Or winding bold chromatics about afflicted shoulders.
Every day the beach gets laid, and little girls 'veronica',
Though George the bull belittles any play for him.
He gets a butterfly-knife for his birthday – yet another blade
Collected for the sake of it – I never see him cut so much
As string. Every day we snorkel in that under-tent,
And foam clouds crevices of urchins or anemones
Where avatars in rubber come to trace the ghosts of fish.
Above the silver lining where *their* element begins,
Harried sand has granules even redder than the fellows
Lagering *paellas* in tavernas under blinds.
People split and wrinkle as the water comes together.
Someone takes apart a parasol as others beach
Their black pneumatic outboard with the single yellow stripe.
And at about this time, within a crimson ring of boards,
A yellow hose is dampening the sand while *pasodobles*
Rallentando right around the tannoy. Poplars taller
Than the stand point shadow spears towards the killing-ground.
Nearly six o'clock by now; and bussing in like us,

Tourists in extreme sombreros pat their loaded wallabies,
Or leap from place like crickets taking photos of themselves,
For the fans are now aflutter in the bull-club of Gerona,
And pennants flurry stripes at the crest of the arena,
As the hose is drawn in and late ones wedged in between
And flexed greys high-step rather lavishly and after
The parade we get the rakers and an orchestra
Ruptures wind haphazardly above a pride of matadors.
In comes the bull at a trot, breaking into charges and
Enlarging from the haunches, though like a barge to turn
When capes on offer swirl away the target for the horn.
They run at him with *banderillas* held flamenco high
Above his shoulders while he tilts quixotically at sails:
Easy to miss, and even if palpable, shaken loose by
An angry toss – who now stands stock still and black
Till the wasp-slim novice in his epaulets removes his cap,
Sweeps the lumbering rush beyond him, sucking ever thinner,
So the sharpness passes very close. And after that,
As the *banderillas* drain the apex of his back,
The bull begins to falter, and his killer knees the sand,
Showing the *muleta* with a debutant vulgarity.
A last rush is mustered, though the head nods in disarray –
The blade sighted, aimed, and shoved between the vertebrae,
The struck beast wafted in circles till he keels aside.
Then the mule-team brings the harness in, and as the fêted
User of the sword freshens up at the side of the ring,
The carcass is connected by its horns that serve as handles,
Dragged around the sand, then dismembered off the scene,
As eagles wheel and circle and continue circling in
A cloud above some natural arena made of crags
Where canine echoes bark inside the rock, or so it seems.
Effortless, their wings ascend, increasingly remote,

As George proceeds to bark back at the wilderness for fun
And small stones roll on our exit from this kettle-drum.
Then once more we pack ourselves as best we can between
Our sleeping-bags, inflatables, knives and sharpened pencils,
Before we start our climb towards the stations of the sun,
Identifying campsites on our longish journey home.

LORNA'S MISTAKES

Can't even squat on the potatoes
And pigs on the loo without banging
As she should. Misreads art instead
Of getting up, her head on the latch
Incessantly. Talks about food in
The wrong direction. Sits on the map and
Points the car off a castle by
Two ants' nests. Falls miles on the
Way to the nudists. Lets the milk boil
Over the rapids backwards. Over
Goes the pan and scorches the carnet.
Loses a rock too late. Gets bit
When she can't pronounce *œufs*.
Sits on my pimples. Can't resist
Watching the bats, then slips
And comes down to read my book
On her bum. Won't settle down
In some ravine. Spills her insignificant
Blisters, plasters all the wine and
Uses all the paper. Can't find
The tent, pisses on her pen. Uses
More onion than she should
And eats her endings at night
With a prickly bush. Can't pronounce
Battles drunkenly. She can't.

MELUSINE

Here, there and everywhere, the deepening green
Of forests: tart scent of resin in the air.
These never-ending pines bring on hypnosis.
Parallel lanes keep flickering to infinity.
Metallic tints corrode each flaking carapace.

We go in search of the most hidden ponds,
Far from all bright parasols, quite off the route
Of any tarmac cycle path; the sands
There, where the snake discards its skin,
Trod only by the Fairy Melusine.

Here, there and everywhere, each placid dune
Deepens our sleep with hints of the Sandman.
Breezes bend her mass to the never-ending
Curve of the ocean. Motherly ways
Of completing things amend each soft relapse.

We drift across her crown, our hardened feet
Engulfed by grains which give underneath us
Leaving ephemeral tracks: they simply
Vanish in an hour or so; restoring ribs
Where pine-cones read as nipples.

Here, there and everywhere, the breakers glint
And steepen ultramarine, splintering
Vague plantations into carbonated spume.
It seems amazing that a thing could make a perfect form
Simply by collapsing on itself.

We sink before its equidistant line.
Close up, the waves choose to hover
Before they come down. Our pleasure then
Beats many another – bravely being
Bowled about like puppies by their mother.

Here, there and everywhere, behind the dune,
By tracks where children cycle at the side
Of jogging mothers, everyday more lean,
The forest breezes murmur of the sea
While breeding pigeons croon for Melusine.

MUTED COLOURS

You might think the apple-tree outside our tent would refer to
  itself as a spider:
It splays its dark limbs like the tortuous hands of an iron Eduardo
  Chillida.
One terrace down, there are birches like slim adolescents; a lissom
  young pair
With washing-lines strung out between them hung as if with their
  own underwear.

Few are the tents here: of these, most are pitched near their cars.
Some under birches, some under willows and some under apples
  like ours.
A camper is tapping in tent-pegs nearby while others bat shuttle-
  cocks up at me.
It has been a milky, insidious day; a day of particular subtlety

When we've been randy then languid by turns; a day when one
  nurses one's brandy
In the hushed atmosphere of a Marquet, or even of a Morandi.
Perhaps I am seeing whatever I see in such painterly terms at
  this time
Because we have just spent an arduous day wandering through
  the Guggenheim:

A day to digest in this dangling cove where the willows keep time
  to the breezes
And little disturbs our congenial retreats, apart from when some-
  body sneezes
In view of a house now incomplete except for its staircase and roof:
Through it I glimpse a bit more of the hill which has kept itself
  blue and aloof.

A large building occupies part of its slope – the hospital, one
 might suppose.
And now, intermittently, one or two sounds travel up from
 the port at my toes,
For it's steeply below; the distant repeat of an outboard, then,
 later, a gull,
Then a while after that the blessedly brief cling-clanging of
 a bell.

It's a din that disguises the quite unobtrusive departure of a
 camper-van
As I survey the unusually calm bay of Biscay with its horizon-
 line
Facing me now just as vertically as the tall pine-trees planted
 a twist
Of the lane below me, though both the sea and the pines
 themselves became lost

In the fog of the morning, fog which has lifted, bequeathing
 this laqueous residue
Which has the power to quieten everything, even the willows.
 I've little to do
But appreciate this – this Vichyssoise – brewed by a storm in
 the high Pyrenees
And then confused by the turquoise fume lifting off bark-
 tattered gum-trees.

The campers are loosening rain-tautened guy-ropes or going
 about those boring
Tasks like inflating mattresses which must always accompany
 touring,
For this was a day of mere drizzle or less; yet a spray which
 defeated their plans
By ruining all the washing strung between willows, birches
 and caravans.

But yuccas and figs and some stunted palms in stout terracotta jars
Border the campsite's convenient café, and even the largest cars
Move peacefully here, with no prangs and no dents, and it is only
    rarely
A car-boot slams with an over-loud bang – for the campers manage
    this fairly.

The sky seems wrapped around them all in suspended immobility.
New arrivals stretch and then head off for some facility
As the shuttlecocks get abandoned now, for the spray returns as
    rain
And the cloudiness thickens and forms a shroud which erases
    things again.

SUMMER'S END

A waitress wanders with a lost *steak frites*.
Fathers nuzzle the ears of their inconsolable idiots.
Tomorrow it is back to the institution.
Meanwhile the ash-blond twins have monopolised
Teddy's Picnic – a fruit-machine for
The under-fives. Most of these
Would kill each other with the coloured balls
If they could. Others kick – carried
Screaming from the field. Really the play-pen
Is the sword of Damocles. It's easy to see
How guilty the exhausted fathers feel
About intruding into it in order to abduct hysterics.
Mothers examine small bottoms and can't
Imagine why the fathers haven't already taken them
To do it. The boat lurches sideways.
A thousand breakfasts go with it.
The screams reach a pitch beyond all registers.
There's nowhere to sit and the idiots
Have fallen in love with their new stereos.
Cripples find their sea-crutches.
Who has stuffed the loo with Mr Flipper?

Tintinnabulum

STEPHANIE

Bathing in the dark, below a cliff.
The sea, so salty, buoys me up.
The others nowhere, hidden now
By surges off to the left;
Muscular Paul, and a slip of a girl
Swimming in her panties.

An old dog, paddling to keep
Afloat, I'm in my groundless
Element; far out, and remote
From cavern meals by lamp–light.
The girl's name is Stephanie.
I could fasten on her like an octopus.

Here is a deep to dive inside.
I come up alone, to ride
These blind troughs the wave rips.
Feathers are a spume on space.
It's clear still, it's as if the night
Were just fixing the star in her other ear.

HEADLANDS

These holiday places with the views prove deserted.
If people ever lived here they are long gone,
Like the inhabitants of a little town
Who have somehow wandered onto an urn
And got stuck there. Except for a cat,
There's no one about to breathe in the air
Or appreciate how each tenacious cone
Endeavours to punctuate sheer azure.
Breezes dance with the sea on their own,
And it goes unobserved how briskly they move.
A dragonfly, setting its sights on some bushes
Rooted sublimely, hangs over the cove,
And the deep repeatedly slathers its tushes,
Then crams the entire coast into its mouth.
If it should swallow now, what would remain,
Apart from one or two swifts and a dove?

THE PINE

Although they may evoke
The sea's fluidity
Or the more elastic
Convulsions of a snake,
These roots, talons of the
Pine, prove adamantine

– Cooled in the initial
Pursuit of delving down.
That each hook's a conduit
Seems scarcely credible,
Considering the rock
They grapple and their own

Iron constitution.
Standing so often close
To the sea's edge, shouldn't
What moisture there is prove
Saline? Maybe it can
Subsist on brine, the pine,

Or wring the very stone
For memory of rain.
Certainly it's able
To grow out of a crack
In some limestone needle,
Its deeply guttered bark

Altering tint, as if
It were made of metal;
Its shape preserving that
Of the young tree it was.
If it should have bent at
Its base to stretch outwards

From an older shadow,
Reaching for some sunlight
Of its own, this action
Leaves its lineament on
That pine when fully grown:
Infancy containing

The makings of a gnarled
Posture in some ancient
Armed with the spikes of dead
Branches. Only in its
Most fervent twigs, where the
Needles sprout, is the pine

In the least changeable.
But with its branches flung
Across the view, as if
Identifying sails,
This Southerner prevails;
Sheltering card-players

And abandoned poses;
Providing a trunk to
Hide behind while watching
Girls who spread the bottoms
Of bikinis before
They dive into the pure

Turquoise below them, or
Lending a toe-hold to
Porphyry-toned boys who leap
From the tallest ledges,
Honouring their pledges
To do so; and the pine,

With its pilot, the small
But garrulous cricket,
Bears witness to their feats,
As it does to the sea's
Less accountable moods
And manifestations.

Certainly it enjoys
Its attachment to the
Mediterranean,
Forming dark arabesques
To frame it, and dancing
A welcome on headlands:

Each an abiding form
Which remarks with its own
Stark figure on the sea's
Abrupt carnivalesques.
However, these wilful
Trees are not disposed to

Secure the best view of
Such drama by crowding
The gallery, rather
Each abstains from too close
Company with neighbours,
Cherishes a certain

Fastidiousness in
Its choice of vantage point,
As if it knew that it
Looks best in silhouette.
This tall one dips its crest,
Spreading a damask shawl

Of shade infused with light
On a shelf designed
For the poem or the tryst;
Its intervals touching
The sensitive page or
The party to be kissed.

RISING FROM THE PINES

The sun becomes a vase,
Then emulates the moon,
Then reverses horns,
Then the vase returns:

A vase without a handle
Tipping out its crimson
To smoke a bit of heaven
As we may use a candle.

LA RENTRÉE

Rejection slips, and dust, and letters of rejection
Or denial; and the hair everywhere, of cats,
Of women long departed, their wistful lingering
In drains, on brushes, in the pale trays of showers

That turn into storms, engulfing every aspect
As the sky goes into labour, thundering its bolts
Above Marseilles. Blenching the ports and a tall basilica,
Striking the forts; soaking shirts, chemises, shorts.

TINTINNABULUM

*'So when one wing can make no way
Two joynéd can themselves dilate.'*
    LORD HERBERT OF CHERBURY

Hung with small bells, his Pompeian charm
Comes with one wing and dangles down,
Called to its turns by the whim of the air.

This haunted noon, strung from a pine,
It practically refuses to revolve at all,
Setting off tremors that would register

Only on the tympanum of a hare;
And yet its less than perceptible chime
Touches him with an imaginary feather,

Inching arousal out of its shell
As far as the long slow head of the snail
Whose rapture is a sort of bradyseism.

MASK

It is like being given the key, finally,
To some empty cupboard – your free entry
To a land made of sky delineated
Simply by pergolas. It is just over
The wall or the wall opposite,
And naturally you live forever there.
All you need do is pass through that door.

HERA

The Goddess steps off a storm-cloud onto the mountain.
She comes breezily down the valley to find her favourite
    temple
A jumble of column drums, oil drums;
And, in the shade of a pine, one fallen metope;
The violence of its subject worn away;
Then murals clawed by graffiti,
And murals, on some blistering journey later,
Executed with spray-guns on the sides of goods yards.
Exhausted bodies in railway compartments
Echo the abandoned poses of catastrophe.
Now she bears down on cadaverous sockets,
Tunnels at night through volcanoes, emerges
Dark as the night that smears its pitch across
Cobbles in alleys where under one massive archway
She must confront that dog from hell:
Magnus the mastiff, sent by the Camorra.
But Asia befriends him, takes off his great spiked collar,
Offers her hand to a slobbering tongue;
For this is what she has become, a super-heroine:
The punk queen, dragging on her spliff
Under the ornate monument to an ascendant Christ.

THE DIVER

An isolated butterfly reiterates the colour
Of a girl's short dress as she threads
Her way through the low stone alleys
Of a labyrinth that once was under water.

She and I have spent a baking holiday
Moving on from one ruined city
To another. The swimming-pool is just a dry
Depression, its one intriguing feature

Being the maze submerged in it. Perhaps
This was covered by a platform for the judges
Of aquatic competitions. Maybe fishes
Sought the gloom underneath its arches.

How little we know about anything. Why,
For instance, has the girl begun to shave
Between her legs, leaving just one tantalising
Tuft – exposing the seams of her thighs?

Does she do it for me, or for her bikini?
The ancients may have needed to contain
Some submarine Minotaur, or they
Made their puzzle simply for its novelty –

Having once hypothesised it. This is how
A lot gets done, I guess. The present is as much
Of an enigma as the past. We are provided
With evidence, yes, but evidence of what?

Certainly the pluvium of that roofless villa
Once caught the rain coming in through its roof;
But in the main we tread a bewildered path
Between edifices with or without walls,

Piecing together the hopelessly frayed mosaics
Of our lives, wondering which way to go
Along roads of good camber made of pentangular stones
Fitted ingeniously together and running with

A clear sense of purpose between some flattened
Properties. The girl teeters on the edge
Of a broken wall just as she did on the ledge
Of a rock by the sea. I told her to go for it then –

To plunge is not to fall. Don't think too much
If you want to experience a fresh element,
As the butterfly said to the chrysalis. Now I help her
To jump down. On Ischia I swam off on my own.

CHEWING HER NAPE

Impossibly randy, reeking of goat,
His wattles hung from a bearded throat,
His extra-terrestial hard-on
Simply too big for Daphnis – or for Daphne.

The one in shrinkage fingers pipes:
As for the other, she's shacked up with a satyr
Or worse, a thing as obscene as a Capuan,
A balding, toothy Sybarite – whereas

She is toothsome herself – tall men
Tend to glare at her. She cannot bear to be spat upon –
Even when it soothes her bites. Does not
Need his bites – raises her sandal against him.

THE OLD AGE OF THE FAUN

My heart isn't in it, what with the foot and mouth;
And given their condition, gay abandon
Better be abandoned. Panic used to seize them.
Now uncouth behaviour is beneath them.

Bring me a tooth-pick as well as a hoof-pick.
These once shaggy knees could do with a transplant.
I feel sympathy for stuffed animals;
The velvet gone from their noses.

My own has been used as a battering ram.
Glorious, but the cause of consternation.
I shall cut back on my afternoons.
No one can take me seriously.

URSULA

Ursula works at a writers' café
In Regensburg – where they've chosen to offer
Literature, dished up with literary food
To suit the occasion – she does the cooking:
I can see her seasoning a bird.

Here, where the vamps with overwrought features
Have been replaced by tourists, and teachers,
Ursula follows you fluently, slick
As anything coating these Argentine reaches.
Cradled now, she sighs as if asleep.

Only the melody happens to matter;
Lengthens the beats of your newly wed hearts.
But Ursula, Christ, it's like dancing with butter.
You're holding a girl who melts in your arms,
Meets another partner and departs.

Each of us feels he's already inside her,
Then the sensation is over, not done;
It would be something to offer an arm
And walk her home through a concretized dawn,
Nicely basted as she'd be by then:

Drenched in a seasoning of her own making;
Flavoured by the fronts of other men.

HONORARY VAMPIRE

The entire day kicks off at night.
Obliged to stalk uncertain streets
In prescription shades I look the part:

The night being darker than the night,
With thunderous traffic of somber
Forces lit by boxes, neon, meters.

Having mislaid my proper specs,
I pass at risk from invisible crosses,
Heading for my rendezvous with shadows:

They slide like cats between my legs,
And later, as a spectral light
Blenches victims dumped in *colectivos*,

I lurch towards my own nocturnal
Refill of voracious dreams;
Coffin hidden jealously by blinds.

AT LA VIRUTA

The music of the spheres may be heard in Buenos Aires,
Where it is just possible to invite heavenly bodies
Onto the floor – for instance, Janina's:
Equine though it be, truth to tell.
I would bet on her to win the National.

ARGENTINA

As if in revenge, the spirit of Sunday invaded the rest of
    the week.
Grills remained locked before fashionable shops;
Cafés kept their chairs stacked, their tables upside down on
    top of others;
And lovers sat on doorsteps like in Mexico.
The parks were full of dog-packs. There was nowhere else
    to go,
And gradually they simply ceased to meet.
Life had retreated from once lively corners:
The city was suffering from a lack of air.
Wads of autumnal bills became thinner than pencils.
The people too: they passed through their acquaintances.
Once they had noticed their friends disappear.
Now everyone was invisible. Nobody jingled. Nothing
Could ever be left for a tip. Faced with a beetroot black
    market,
Moonlighting did a midnight flit.
Work played rather more than hard to get.
And just as a reef left high and dry bleaches into stone,
Everything died. The government closed down.
Carnal relations were put aside by a deflowered economy.
Rather than being out and about, you took to a siesta on
    your sofa,
Dealing with this fiscal drought by dreaming –
Of trills registering the liquidity of tills,
Rivers of customers, rows of identical fruit
Producing cash flow, till your worries spoilt the show;
Each unsubstantiated fount evaporating as swiftly
As immigrant ambitions – they were queuing to go home –
For other than its echo in a name, its suggestion in the moon
And the glitter in a sequin or a tear,
There was never any silver to be found here.

BEVERLEY AT IGUAZÚ

Her father had diarrhea:
He didn't care to start
The available trails
In case he got caught short.
The onomatopoeia
Of the falls was lost on him.

Anyway his heart
Was in no condition
To climb the higher trail
Or to get back up
To the Sheraton
From the lower one.

He preferred to stew
On their balcony,
Whiskey in hand,
Feeling he owned
The incredible view
He'd paid to see.

A little train
Had set them down
By the cat-walk
That led to the void.
He hadn't enjoyed
Getting soaked to the skin

As the wide upper river
Flung itself over
The edge into vapour
Brewed in the Devil's Throat:
Garganta del Diablo.
Ok, he said, let's go.

She gloried in the sight,
And in the seeming-slow
Swags of sunlit heaviness
Falling into sheer white
Nothingness whose glow
Suffused her emptiness

And came billowing back
To saturate the spirit
As much as the clothes,
While she stared into it,
Stunned by a chariot
Drawn by a thousand hooves.

He merely found it loud.
She thought it *the* place
To commit suicide.
You'd better wipe your face:
It's ruined your mascara,
Her father replied.

But it was the best brink
She'd ever been brought to,
And while he used the john
In their luxurious room,
She went off alone,
Overwhelmed by its boom;

Astonished that meanderings
Could end in so much turmoil,
Where there were vultures too
Who cleansed their wings
By spiralling towards the clouds
On each humid thermal.

She got invaded by dreams
Of drinking at giant taps,
And following the maps
In the brochures,
Came closer to the vultures
By being ferried across

To a densely jungled bay
In the midst of various chutes.
She met one corpulent lizard
Who scuttled away
To his undergrowth home,
Leaving her to roam,

And later she bathed
In the cool shallows
Of the lower river.
An infinite number
Of curious minnows
Nibbled her throat there.

Under the water,
She loosened her brassiere.
Papa would have frowned:
For what could be crazier
Than this daughter
Of his freeing her breasts,

In order for these
To be eaten by fishes?
They should rid the waterways
Of the little pests.
Ah, but what lovely,
Lovely breasts!

As the Englishman,
Who had danced
A tango with her in
Buenos Aires,
Had called them
When, entranced,

He gently pressed
That part of her
Closer against him,
Moving her with his chest,
Till she seemed to swim
In his element.

The night was terrible.
She found it quite impossible
To sleep or to give vent
To her feelings as
She lay prone
In the bed next to her father's one.

The Sheraton was located
Within the National Park
That closed each evening
At seven o'clock.
The air conditioning
Worked too well:

Its all-devouring roar
Was louder than the falls
That never ceased to spout
And bathed the moon in vapour.
She needed to explore
While no one was about;

But this was strictly
Prohibited by
The authorities,
And anyway
It was dangerous out there,
What with the puma's lair

And that of the jaguar
Somewhere close
In the sub-tropical mass
Of bromeliad and liana,
Densities of grass
And palmetto

Hemmed in by
A precipice
Made treacherous
By numberless cascades
Into canebrakes
Seething with snakes.

Her father kept getting up
And staggering to
The lavatory.
She had to get away
But was clearly in no
Position to do so.

All she could do
Was fret the hours through,
And pace up and down,
Up and down,
On their balcony
Under the moon.

INTERRUPTIONS

Halfway into your body
And the family gets back:
Adjusted, we emerge from the settee.

Your mother has to endure my peck,
Her hands being full of lettuces.
But we can't help it, she and I,

We both see my deposit
On her stomach in the month of May,
A week or so before she met your father.

I know she'd rather not see it,
Prefers me near the antipodes,
As I am, waking slowly from

This unsatisfactory dream
To work up lines about goals
In my untidy room.

That's the football here – it's rife.
How different things are with sex,
Where a near miss is what I've been

Aiming for, baby, most of my life.

DANCING EMPANADAS

Sharpen knives by pedalling the grinder attached to your bike.
There is going to be a showdown today,
If you're free after yesterday's showdown.
But will it be ok to leave my saucepan in the cloakroom?

Corralitos cannot close *milongas*, and on balmy nights
Orquestas play in theatre streets
Where tango parties clash with demonstrations.
The crisis is confusing also for *porteños*,

Which is why the pigs bring out their hoses,
Yes, but fireworks squirt back,
While on one loud corner some life-sized *empanadas*
Occupy the zebra, strumming on their placards.

You could suffocate inside a Cornish pasty too, I guess,
But in this heat it's a dead-end source of income.
Being a threatened jaguar for Green Peace can't be better though,
Nor can spinning parasols in blimpish pairs of overalls

As the fiesta skips, hops, jumps along the street
In silk tails and top-hats, t-shirts embroidered with tongues.
Turn off Duhalde. Put on D'Arrienzo.
I understand the custom is to go down, dancing, with the ship.

MIRRORS IN THE ZOO

'Mira, un girafe!' Not to be outdone,
Some stupid git of a brother pipes up,
'Mira, una paloma!' as a
Vein in the forehead throbs
To the p–pulsation of a toothache.

Meanwhile the puma is in ill humour
And everything goes the colour
Of its background as I wobble on,
In my pain ungainly as the polar bear
– An anomaly here –

The climate too exotic
To accommodate that fur, and the poor
Beast looking as near extinction
As the condor is – and as I feel.
Why did I put that spider in my mouth?

Now I can't get rid of it.
Have I enough aspirin to last
Till the black panther
Emerges out of its shadow?
I don't think so.

Knotted snakes coagulate in forks.
Oh, I'm too crook to appreciate
The white tiger stretching like a yogi.
Look at the llamas! What terrible,
Terrible teeth!

AMIABLY

There she was, in the flophouse, with her trick.
But so what? No need to get uptight.
He simply told the punk to beat it quick.
To pick on *him* just wouldn't have been right.

Later, with his slippers brought, at ease,
As if he didn't care or hadn't seen her
At it, he got holed up with his squeeze,
And called out, Steep the *maté*, Catalina!

She served him, in a lather of humility,
While he enjoyed a well-earned cigarette,
Offered her his usual idle chat . . .

Bestowed on her a kiss more like a prayer;
And then, with an incredible tranquillity,
Used thirty-four thrusts, amiably, to slay her.

From the Spanish of Iván Diez

NOTES

GRUMUS MERDAE An expression sometimes used to describe the tendency among burglars to defecate very obviously on the premises they break into.

ROSSIANA Dedicated to Tino Rossi, the French singer, hailing from Corsica, who sang a few tangos and several waltzes. Because he sang in French, his accompaniment was an accordion rather than the bandoneon favoured in Argentina.

ANDANTE MODERATO *Milonga* is the name for one of the dances in the tango's 'family' of dances. It is also the word used for a night dancing the tango in a salon.

KNICKERS The poem refers to the work of John Kacere, the Lebanese artist who painted in New York, a pioneer of photo-realism.

BEAUTONIA This was written in Serbia, in the spring of 1996, at Fantast Castle in Vojvodina, built by the Dumdjerski family in the 1920s.

PROGRESS This is, or was, the name of the State Department Store in Serbia.

CANCELLED FLIGHTS When I first visited the Ardèche in the eighties there were some 60 pairs of Bonfili eagles flying above the gorge. Today, there are none.

BRIDGE The poem refers to le Pont d'Arc, a natural bridge of stone close to the recently discovered Chauvet cave, which contains some striking prehistoric paintings.

MASK The walled garden depicted on one wall of the Roman villa at Oplontis, near Naples, is mirrored by that on the opposite wall.

THE DIVER The labyrinth in a swimming-pool can be seen at Paestum, some forty miles south of Naples.

URSULA   In this poem I have attempted to evoke the rhythm of the tango.

HONORARY VAMPIRE   *Colectivos* are the cheap buses in Buenos Aires.

DANCING EMPANADAS   The *corralito* is the term for the law that prevents people in Argentina from taking more than one thousand pesos per month out of their bank account. *Porteños* are natives of Buenos Aires. *Empanadas* are pasties filled with meat, vegetables or cheese.

Anthony Howell

Anthony Howell was born in 1945. After an early spell dancing with the Royal Ballet, he decided to concentrate on poetry and performance art. In 1973 he was invited to the International Writing Program in Iowa and in 1974 he founded The Theatre of Mistakes, a performance company which made notable appearances at the Cambridge Poetry Festival, The Paris Biennale and the Hayward Gallery as well as in New York. He has published eight previous books of poetry and a novel. He has also received major bursaries from the Arts Councils of England and Wales, and was shortlisted for a Paul Hamlyn Award. He has recently returned from Buenos Aires where he was enabled to improve his tango by a grant from London Arts.